DEFINITIVE GUIDE FOR MEANS OF PAYMENT AND INTERNATIONAL FINANCING

JOSE-NICANOR PINILLA
BARCELONA

DEDICATION

Special dedication to my wife Ana Miriam and my sons Joel and Noah. For more information: www.escueladelemprendedor.com

CONTENTS

ACKNOWLEDGEMENTS

To all the teachers I have had since 1989, when international trade in Spain was not taken into account in the universities. Especially to the precursors of these subjects in Aragon, the International Business School (CESTE) and the University of Wales. I am grateful to all the students I have had for more than 20 years, who have taught me how to teach this subject. Thanks to the support of the School of the Entrepreneur, many teachers and professionals will be able to publish our knowledge in different business management subjects.

1.EXPORTING AND INVESTING

In the context of the internationalisation of the economy, investments abroad constitute economic movements to which the tax system does not remain impassive. On the other hand, they are positive factors for economic growth, and companies benefit from corporate tax incentives, subject to the fulfilment of certain requirements. Any investment is likely to generate income flows, i.e. **repatriation of profits**, which will be taxed. As a general rule, taxation takes place where the investment is made, but also where the investing company resides. A **double taxation** problem arises. Each state unilaterally sets its own tax rules to avoid double taxation. In OECD member countries, as in other third countries, a bilateral mechanism has been developed to avoid double taxation.

1.1. DEDUCTIONS FOR INVESTMENT ABROAD

Before making an investment abroad, a company should consider whether there are tax incentives to do so because, if there are, the return will be higher than expected.

> It also includes 25% of the costs of promotion and advertising of multi-year projection for the launch of products and the opening and prospecting of markets abroad, including attendance at international trade fairs held in Spain. In the event that subsidies are received, the taxable base will be reduced by 65% of the amounts received.

☐ **Deduction for investments related to export activities.** This is a deduction from the corporate income tax liability of the investing company. They constitute 25% of investments abroad in the creation of branches or the acquisition or creation of subsidiaries in which at least 25% of the shareholding is held in export-related activities, except financial or insurance activities. If the 25% shareholding is reached in stages over time, the deduction will be applied on the basis of the investment made in the year in which it is reached and in the two preceding years. Once the right to apply the deduction has been obtained, article 44 of the tax law establishes certain limits to its imputation in the year. However, if such limits apply, the part of the deduction not taken in the year may be used in the following ten years.

- **Deduction for investments for the establishment of companies abroad.** Investments in subsidiaries abroad will entitle the investor company to defer taxation of its profits by an amount equivalent to the amount invested, if certain requirements are met:

- The investment in the equity of the non-resident subsidiary must give a majority of the voting rights.
- The subsidiary must carry on business activities other than financial, insurance, real estate or the provision of services to related entities resident in Spain.
- The subsidiary must not be resident in the European Union or in a tax haven.
- The activity of the subsidiary must not have been previously carried on under another ownership.
- These requirements must be maintained for at least four years.

The amount equivalent to the amount invested will be deducted from the tax base of the tax year in which the investment was made and may be included in equal parts in the tax base of the following four tax years: the maximum annual amount of the deferred tax base will be 30,050,605.22 euros, without exceeding 25% of the tax base prior to the calculation of the deferral.

☐ **Allowance for impairment of financial goodwill.** When a company buys the shares of another company and pays more for them than the book value of the related assets and liabilities, the excess constitutes financial goodwill that reflects the purchaser's favourable expectations. But such goodwill is an intangible asset whose long-term value is uncertain, so it would be prudent to write it off over time as if it were a loss. Writing it off as a loss reduces the annual profit of the investing company, and therefore the corporate income tax it will have to pay.

> Thus, the allocation made by Spanish companies for the depreciation of financial goodwill, up to a limit of 5% per year, on acquisitions of equities of non-resident entities in Spain, will be a deductible expense.

1.2. TAX COMPARISON BETWEEN BRANCH AND SUBSIDIARY

Once the investment has been made, a number of income flows from the foreign company to the parent company are to be expected: dividends, royalties, management support services, trade in goods or services incorporating so-called "transfer prices" (prices different from normal market prices), capital gains may arise and sometimes even staff may be seconded from the parent company to the foreign company.

The branch of a company could be defined as: A secondary establishment, without its own legal personality; with the same corporate purpose as its parent company; with an independent physical establishment; with a permanent representative in charge of management; which is subordinate to the directives of its parent company, without autonomy in terms of assets and liabilities with respect to the latter.

Let us understand that opening branches does not imply the creation of a new company. It is not an entity with its own autonomy and distinct from the "head office" (company or self-employed person) that generates it, so it will not have its own name, distinct from that of the main establishment. In any case, the incorporation of a branch must be formalised in a public deed and registered in the Commercial Register.

Unlike branches, subsidiaries are trading companies, with their own legal personality and distinct from their parent company, with their own articles of association, governing and administrative bodies.

It could be said that they are separate and distinct from the main entity, only created by the main entity, which is its founder and which we will call the "parent". And being a separate entity (owned by the parent, but distinct from it), they may go their separate ways in the future, if the parent sells its shares in the subsidiary. For this reason, an essential difference in liability arises from the above: The liability of the branch is not separate from that of the legal entity that creates it. It is the same, as the branch is an extension of the "head office" and they share the legal personality of the main establishment. And therefore they also share liability.

On the other hand, the subsidiary, being a person independent from the parent company and endowed with full personality, i.e. true legal autonomy, also has independence in liability matters.

What is the same as the branch is that the subsidiary must also be created by public deed and registered in the Commercial Register. Like all commercial companies.

Loss-making investments. It may also happen that the company domiciled abroad makes losses. In the same way that positive income obtained abroad has an impact on the Spanish taxation of the parent company when it arrives in Spain, so too will negative income or losses, which will reduce the profit and loss account with corporation tax.

□ *If it is a branch*: as it has no legal personality and constitutes a single person with the parent company, its negative results are automatically incorporated, with a negative sign, into those of the parent company, with the consequent reduction and lower corporation tax liability.

□ *Subsidiary*: the impact is not automatic, but will depend on whether the accounting regulations allow the corresponding provision to be made for impairment of the investment, which will only occur if, after the loss suffered, the book value of the foreign investment falls below that which it had at the time of its initial materialisation. This will not occur if, in previous years, the subsidiary made undistributed profits and the current year's losses do not exceed the amount of these undistributed profits because, despite the fall, the value of the foreign subsidiary will still be higher than its initial historical value.

Taxation of personnel posted abroad. If the investment abroad is accompanied by the sending of personnel from Spain to work in the foreign company, it will be useful to analyse the taxation of investing in human assets. We must first analyse the concept of "*habitual residence*": if they continue to receive part of their salary in Spain, they will be taxed here under the general regime for non-residents (withholding tax of 25%), without prejudice to the existence of an international double taxation agreement.

A person is resident in Spain if:

- ➢ Stays 183 days per calendar year
- ➢ That their main professional or business activities are based in Spain
- ➢ When the spouse and children live in Spain and are dependent on him/her.
- ➢ If the transfer of residence to a tax haven takes place, the status of Spanish personal income taxpayer will not be lost in that year and in the following 4 years.

> Excess payments, if the relocation is limited in time, are computed as "per diems exempt from taxation" for Personal Income Tax purposes. If you are going to relocate for a long period of time, you must notify the tax authorities and you will be taxed as non-resident income and not on account of personal income tax.

The subsidiary will be taxed in the source state for corporate income tax on the profit earned and subsequent dividend distributed, plus a withholding tax. But services between the parent and its subsidiary can change this pattern. Services received and paid for by the subsidiary are a deductible expense and reduce its profit, in addition to corporate income taxation.

Profit transfer formulas. The most frequent operations are:

- ✓ Technical assistance, paid for by fees.
- ✓ Administrative management support services.
- ✓ Interest-bearing loans.

They can also sell products, applying the transfer pricing policy, selling to the subsidiary at prices below or above market prices, in accordance with the tax strategy that is in their best interest, always without violating customs regulations regarding the customs value of the goods.

Holding companies. Holding companies that hold the shares of the group's subsidiaries. The main advantage is that they allow deferral of taxation in the State of destination of the income from their investments abroad. Indeed, if the profits were not repatriated and reinvested, their taxation would have been deferred indefinitely. They should be located in countries with double taxation treaties, not in tax havens, which do not have such treaties, so that the dividends or capital gains reach the holding company with little or no taxation at source.

Trademark and patent companies. Many multinationals set up companies in tax havens that own their intangibles, thus delaying taxation in the parent state as long as the funds are not transferred.

> They are assigned by way of **royalties** to another patent and trademark company set up for this purpose. These payments are deductible and are not taxed at source, or only slightly. They are not taxed in the country either, as the royalty expenses paid are offset against the royalties collected.

2. VAT ON INTRA-COMMUNITY TRANSACTIONS

The creation of the Common Market in the EU on 1 January 1993 led to the abolition of tax frontiers and the abolition of border controls. The structural problems and differences between the Member States, due to the different tax rates, have been decisive in the transitional period. This regime, for four years, has become indefinite. The taxation of VAT on intra-Community transactions is based on the following basic principles:

The articulation of the taxable event in the intra-Community acquisition of goods: the abolition of fiscal borders means that imports between Member States will disappear, but the application of the principle of taxation at destination requires the articulation of this taxable event as a technical solution enabling tax to be levied in the Member State of arrival of the goods.

Exemptions for intra-Community supplies of goods: it is important to delimit the exemptions for supplies of goods that are sent from one State to another in order to avoid situations of non-taxation or double taxation in the economic operation that begins in one State and ends in the other.

> They shall be exempt from tax where they are dispatched from one Member State to another, to the customer, who must be a taxable person or a legal person acting as such. In other words, the supply at source will be exempt when it results in a taxable intra-Community acquisition at destination, in accordance with the status of the customer.

Transport as a fundamental service in intra-Community transactions: the exemption of the supply at source and the taxation of the acquisition at destination are conditional on the goods being transported from one Member State to another. Transport in intra-Community trade is treated as a separate operation from supplies and acquisitions and, unlike under the previous legislation, *is not exempt from tax*, although on the whole this taxation system is better because the tax paid can be deducted and the difficulties involved in justifying the exemption are avoided. This transport must be justified with the appropriate consignment note, air or sea bill of lading, CMR, etc.

Harmonisation of import VAT: it is fully harmonised, as it is included in what is known as CUSTOMS DEBT, albeit with the exceptions referring to the rates of import VAT levied in each State.

Taxable event: Article 13 of the Law provides that intra-Community acquisitions are taxable if they are made for valuable consideration. If it is an exchange or barter, there are two exempt supplies and two taxable acquisitions at the same time. The acquisitions must be made by businessmen, not by private individuals, the latter cannot deduct the tax borne, they would only be affected by the difference in rates that may exist between the two States.

Excluded acquisitions: the following are not considered to be intra-Community acquisitions:

- ✓ Where the transferor is exempt from VAT in the Member State. This does not exist in Spain.
- ✓ Acquisitions of goods whose delivery has been taxed under the special regime for second-hand goods, objets d'art, antiques and collectors' items.
- ✓ Acquisitions of goods corresponding to deliveries of goods to be installed or assembled.
- ✓ Distance selling purchases.
- ✓ Excise duty purchases
- ✓ Acquisitions the supply of which in the State of origin of the dispatch or transport was exempt from tax as a deemed transaction

Non-subject acquisitions: Article 14 of the Law contains non-subject acquisitions which are exceptions to the general taxation rules. They require, for their application, a subjective and an objective requirement.

- *Subjective requirement:* types of persons (e.g. taxable persons under the special scheme for agriculture, livestock and fisheries).
- *Objective requirement:* limit of transactions (not exceeding €10,000 in the previous year). The non-taxation will apply to the current year until the acquisitions reach the above-mentioned quantitative threshold.

Exemptions: Article 25 covers exemptions for supplies of goods to other Member States and Article 26 covers exemptions for intra-Community acquisitions of goods as such. The following supplies are excluded from the taxable event:

- ✓ Intra-Community supplies in general, taxable at destination or in the territory of the customer
- ✓ Intra-Community supplies of new intra-Community means of transport to occasional taxable persons
- ✓ Duty-free shop deliveries to travellers on intra-Community flights and crossings
- ✓ Intra-Community supplies of second-hand goods, works of art, antiques and collectors' items not subject to the special scheme

✓ Transactions treated as intra-Community supplies of goods In intra-Community acquisitions:
✓ Intra-Community acquisitions of goods the supply of which within the territory of the tax territory would in any case have been non-taxable or exempt
✓ Intra-Community acquisitions of goods the importation of which would, in any case, have been exempt from duty
✓ Intra-Community acquisitions of goods in respect of which the purchaser is entitled to a full refund of the tax due on them.

Taxable base, rates and taxable person: The taxable base is set out in Article 82 of the VAT Law, for the amount of the consideration to be paid by the purchaser, and the rules contained in Articles 79 and 80 on the modification and determination of this base are applicable. The rates coincide with the general rates established in Articles 90 and 91 of the Law, and consist of a standard rate of 16%, a reduced rate of 7% and a super-reduced rate of 4%, which will be applied to intra-Community acquisitions according to the same criteria as those applied in the general VAT system. The taxable person will always be the purchaser of the goods and the law refers to Article 71.

Operation of an intra-Community acquisition:

✓ The Spanish company must obtain the intra-Community VAT number prior to the transaction, registering in the Register of Intra-Community Operators, in accordance with Ministry of Finance Order 2567/2003 section 7, although the AEAT is obliged to include VAT taxpayers who in the previous 12 months have made intra-Community deliveries or acquisitions of goods subject to this tax. Once you have been registered, you will inform your customer or supplier.
✓ The EC supplier issues an invoice for the amount of the transaction, exclusive of VAT.
✓ The Spanish company receives the goods and must now charge VAT to itself as a taxable person.

VAT in international invoicing:

Intra-Community supplies: of movable tangible goods, the vendor must issue a VAT-exempt invoice. As the self-invoice no longer exists for purchasers as of 1 January 2004, the following procedure must be followed: an entry must be made in the invoice register book and the purchase must be recorded with "deductible VAT on intra-Community transactions" for the settlement of the corresponding period. *In the case of invoices for the provision of services, the vendor must also issue the invoice without VAT and the purchaser must issue a self-invoice referring to the invoice number of the intra-Community vendor of the service and proceed with the self-recording of VAT on the invoice. The VAT due under the general scheme must be entered on the document in the VAT return for the period.*

Transactions with third countries: in the case of export invoices, they are exempt from VAT, as VAT is not applicable to shipments to third countries outside the EU. They must be included in the book corresponding to the invoices issued. In the case of third country suppliers, they are exempt from VAT.

VAT on intra-Community supplies of services. The intra-Community aspect of services is not specifically regulated. Only paragraph 2 of Article 70(2) of the VAT Law mentions the regulation of services. The so-called "inversion of the taxable person" takes place, since it is the recipient who will have to self-assess the tax in order to subsequently deduct the amounts paid. The VAT must be shown on the return document as accrued VAT under the general system, while it must be deducted in the box corresponding to deductible VAT on domestic transactions, in accordance with the aforementioned reverse charge rule. These include:

- ✓ Assignments and concessions of copyrights
- ✓ Transfer or grant of goodwill
- ✓ Business management
- ✓ Advertising services
- ✓ Professional advisory and similar services
- ✓ Data processing by computerised procedures
- ✓ Provision of information (transfer of databases)
- ✓ Non-exempted insurance transactions
- ✓ Leasing of movable tangible property, with the exception of means of transport and containers.

> **With regard to the rule on the location of the place of business of the recipient of the service**, Article 70 provides that "if the above services are provided between entrepreneurs or professionals established in the EU, the place of taxation shall be the place of business of the recipient of the service, and these services shall not be taxed in Spain when they are provided by an entrepreneur or professional established in Spain, and the recipient is an entrepreneur or individual resident outside the territory of the EU".

In relation to VAT on transport services, we must distinguish between three activities:

☐ Intra-Community transport: is considered to be carried out in the territory of application of the tax when the transport begins in that territory, unless the recipient of the transport has communicated to the transporter a VAT identification number allocated by another Member State. Also when the transport begins in another State, but the recipient of the service has communicated to the transporter a VAT identification number issued by the Spanish Administration.

☐ <u>Services ancillary to transport</u>: when they are physically supplied in that territory, unless the recipient has notified the supplier of the service of a VAT identification number allocated to another State. Also if they have been physically supplied in another Member State, but the recipient has communicated to the supplier of the service an identification number for tax purposes allocated by the Spanish Administration.

☐ <u>Mediation services in intra-Community transport</u>: these services will be subject to VAT at the place where the transport begins and at the place of the recipient of the service who has notified the supplier of the service if he has an intra-Community VAT number.

2.1. VAT ON TRANSACTIONS WITH THIRD COUNTRIES

Article 18 of the LIVA defines importation as "the physical entry of goods into the territory of application of the tax". Therefore, they can only be goods, not services. The goods do not have to be Community goods nor do they have to have been released for free circulation in another Member State against payment of the corresponding import duties.

Taxable event and exemptions. In EU countries there are exempted areas into which goods may enter without payment of import duties and VAT. These areas, as well as various import duty suspension regimes, are set out in Articles 23 and 24 of the LIVA. In these cases, importation will take place when the goods located in these exempted areas or linked to these suspension regimes leave these areas or are unlinked to these regimes. In the case of imports destined for a Member State other than the State of entry of the goods, two cases are established:

➤ When goods arrive in the EU under the T-1 external Community transit procedure, the import takes place in the Member State where the transit is finalised.
➤ Where the goods do not arrive under the transit procedure, the importation for free circulation takes place in the Member State of entry and the dispatch to the Member State of destination takes place through an intra-Community operation of exempt supply and subject acquisition.

<u>*In the aforementioned article 27 of the LIVA, exemptions are included*</u>:

✓ Exemptions for final imports of duty-free goods. For example, personal goods in a removal, imports under the travellers' regime, low-value goods.
✓ Exemption for imports of fishery products

✓ Exemptions for imports of goods under diplomatic or consular arrangements and for imports of goods for international organisations
✓ Technical exemptions, e.g. those established to avoid double taxation.
✓ Taxable base, rates and taxable person. The taxable amount of imports is set out in Article 83 of the LIVA and is made up of the customs value of the imported products, determined in accordance with the GATT valuation code set out in the Community Customs Code, in Articles 29 to 32, and defined as "*the **transaction value**, the price actually paid or payable for the imported goods (normally the invoice price) agreed between the seller and the buyer*". To this value must be added a series of ancillary costs that form part of the import operation:
✓ Sales commissions.
✓ Cost of packaging and packing.
✓ Transport, loading and insurance costs to the place of entry of the goods into Community territory.
✓ Fees and licence fees that the buyer is obliged to pay as a condition of sale to the seller to be integrated into the imported products.

✓ Shares in the price of resale, transfer or use of the imported goods, which are recognised or reversed in favour of the seller. Once the customs value has been determined by the appropriate method, the following items must be added for the determination of the taxable amount for VAT on imports:
- Taxes, duties, levies and other charges: customs duties, excise duties due on importation, agricultural levies and other import charges provided for in the Common Agricultural Policy and any charges due on importation
- Ancillary costs such as commission, packing, transport and insurance costs incurred up to the first place of destination in the EU. The first place of destination shall mean the place shown on the consignment note or any other document covering the entry of the goods into the EU.

In general, the importer is always a taxable person, regardless of whether or not he is an entrepreneur and regardless of the purpose for which the imported goods are intended, whether for private consumption or an economic activity. Importers are also considered to be travellers, RENFE, when acting on behalf of third parties by virtue of international agreements, Chamber of Commerce with ATA carnets, Customs Agents, when acting in their own name and on behalf of their principals, are subsidiarily liable for the payment of the tax.

☐ **Operational**. The process for calculating the import VAT liability:

1. Find the taxable amount of import duties, including ancillary costs.
2. Calculate the share of customs duties or excise duties, depending on whether the goods are subject to duty or excise duties.
3. Calculate the taxable amount for import VAT on the basis of the customs value.

4. Add items that are not included in the tax base.

5. Apply the respective rates to obtain the amount of import VAT.

2.2. VAT ON TRANSACTIONS TREATED AS IMPORTS

Operations assimilated to importation are considered to be the exit from the exempt areas or the abandonment of the suspensive regimes of goods whose delivery or intra-Community acquisition to be introduced into the aforementioned areas or linked to the said regimes would have benefited from the exemption established in 36.1 of the LIVA or would have been the object of deliveries or provision of services also exempted by the aforementioned articles.

These are always goods originating in the EU whose internal supply or intra-Community acquisition was exempt due to their destination in an exempt area or under a duty suspension arrangement, and therefore the abandonment of these situations means that, in order to re-establish the neutrality of the tax, the exit is recorded as a transaction treated as an import. Exits of goods from third countries or territories are not included, as such exits constitute importation in the strict sense of the term.

- Taxable base, rates and taxable person. The taxable amount will be that of the last exempt transaction, with the addition of expenses and services carried out under the schemes considered exempt. The rates will be the same as for domestic VAT, i.e. those set out in Articles 90 and 91 of the VAT Law. According to 72.2, the time at which transactions treated as imports are deemed to have been carried out is the time at which the circumstances indicated in each case occur.

- Operation. Let's look at an example to see how it works: a Spanish company based in Barcelona acquires a series of goods in Germany: 100 shirts at €5 and brings them into Spain in a warehouse other than the customs warehouse. The German company invoices the €500 without VAT and the Spanish company, instead of carrying out the steps foreseen for intra-Community acquisitions, does the following:

- You present a simplified SAD to the Customs control office, which will be the nearest to your warehouse other than the customs warehouse, in order to be authorised to enter that warehouse

- No self-refunding of VAT takes place.

- He sells 10 of the shirts in Spain to a customer in Zaragoza and carries out the following operations: He invoices the customer in Zaragoza at 7€ per shirt and produces an invoice for 70€ plus 21% VAT which he will pay on a form 300 as VAT accrued under the general system Of the 100 shirts, only 90 remain. He must now declare the VAT assimilated to the import. He fills in form 380 to pay the assimilated VAT on the 10 shirts, the taxable amount of this VAT assimilated to importation being €50 (€5 X 10 shirts). The corresponding rate, in this case 21%, is applied to this base to obtain the tax liability.

2.3. DOCUMENTS TO BE SUBMITTED

- ✓ Intra-Community transactions
- ✓ Form 036 for registering in the census
- ✓ Declaration form, monthly or quarterly, depending on the company's total volume of operations.
- ✓ Form 349 covering intra-Community transactions, only of movable tangible tangible goods, both delivery and acquisition, excluding services acquired or rendered.
- ✓ Corresponding Intrastat model if above threshold
- ✓ Import operations
- ✓ At customs, the SAD. VAT must be paid using form 031 issued by the import customs office.
- ✓ The deduction of import VAT by means of the monthly or quarterly form
- ✓ ***Transactions assimilated to importation:*** form 380. The deduction of the assimilated VAT is made on the same form 380.

3. INTERNATIONAL MEANS OF PAYMENT

Any international commercial transaction requires a series of prior premises to be established, such as means of payment and bank guarantees. The insecurity of collection means that both the importer and the exporter must be cautious when choosing a secure collection system. For all these reasons, simple and documentary means of payment have been created.

3.1. SIMPLE MEANS OF PAYMENT

Each operation that we are going to carry out in international trade requires an individualised study of the importer's commercial risks, country risk, in order to decide on a transfer, a bank cheque or a simple remittance. It is essential to analyse the confidence we have in our customer. Let us look at the main simple means of payment:

3.1.1. BANK CHEQUE

It is the security issued by a financial institution against its own funds, which implies a payment in favour of a beneficiary. It involves:

- **Ordering party.** A natural or legal person who instructs the drawee bank to issue the cheque.
- **Drawing or issuing bank.** Bank issuing the cheque.
- **Drawee or payer bank.** Foreign correspondent bank of the issuing bank that is to make the payment. Sometimes it is the same issuing bank.
- **Beneficiary.** Natural or legal person to whom the amount of the cheque is paid.

The bank cheque works as follows:

- ✓ **Issue of the cheque.** The payer goes to a bank or savings bank branch or to the Foreign Department and fills in a Payment Order Request form, marking the bank cheque option. The office forwards the request to the Overseas Department, which issues the cheque in euros or another currency according to the instructions on the request and debits the customer's account. The cheque is delivered to the payer directly or through the branch.
- ✓ **Delivery of the bank cheque to the beneficiary.** The payer delivers the bank cheque in person or by registered or express mail to the foreign payee, fulfilling his obligation to make the payment.
- ✓ **Clearing and cashing of the cheque.** The beneficiary, a foreign exporter, presents the bank cheque to his bank.
- ✓ The exporter's bank presents the cheque to the drawee bank whose name and address appear on the bank cheque. The drawee bank, after verifying that the cheque is correct, credits the exporter's bank, and debits the account it has in common with the bank issuing the bank cheque. Banks use the same collection management systems for both bank cheques and personal cheques. They are as follows:
- ✓ **Discount or Negotiation.** In this case, the bank pays the cheque directly to the payee, minus commissions if any, before clearing the cheque with the drawee bank. To speed up cheque collection and avoid sending cheques individually, cash letter agreements are signed with a bank in each country, normally to which all collected cheques are sent for collection.

> There is a risk for the exporter's bank, which is why it is paid to the customer "except for good order", although as it is a bank cheque, the security of collection is greater than with personal cheques, as it is the issuing bank that pays, with greater solvency than a company or individual that may run out of funds.

✓ **Collection management.** The exporting bank will now wait to collect the amount of the cheque and, once it is in its possession, pay it to its client who is the beneficiary of the cheque, minus any commissions, if any. The exporter will take longer to cash the cheque, but the exporting bank assumes no risk. Cheques are normally honoured within two to six days, depending on amounts and currencies. Cheques presented to foreign financial institutions are also cashed.

<u>The bank cheque has a number of advantages and disadvantages</u>:

In terms of benefits:

➢ An important advantage is the security it provides compared to a personal cheque. A bank cheque will always have funds, which reduces the risk of non-payment to the solvency of the bank.
➢ In addition, its collection process is quicker and more accessible than the personal cheque.
➢ Its cost is lower than other documentary means of payment, such as remittances or documentary credits.

With regard to the drawbacks:

➢ Bank cheques take longer to clear than other means of payment such as bank transfers.
➢ There is a risk of loss due to loss or theft of the bank cheque, or of forgery.

3.1.2. TRANSFERS

A bank transfer, also called a simple payment order, is a payment made by the importer's bank to the exporter's bank, which credits the funds to the account of its collecting customer. This form of payment is made by electronic means, the most commonly used being the SWIFT system. The SWIFT network brings together the vast majority of the world's banks and enables fast and secure communication between them.

It involves:

- ✓ **Payer.** This is the importer or payer. He instructs his bank to request the issuance of the transfer to be charged to his account.
- ✓ **Sending bank.** Receives instructions from the originator, checks them and, if deemed appropriate, issues the transfer via the swift interbank communication system.
- ✓ **Correspondent bank.** When the transfer is made in a currency other than that of the country of the issuing bank, the intervention of a bank located in the country of the same currency as the transfer is required. Correspondents are also used when there are no direct clearing systems between the issuing bank and the paying bank.
- ✓ **Paying bank.** This is the bank where the payee holds the account to which the transfer money arrives.
- ✓ **Beneficiary.** Collector or exporter. Receives the funds in his account.

The way the transfer works is as follows:

Application for the payment order. The importer requests the issuance of the transfer from his financial institution by completing a payment order request form.

The following data must be provided:

- ✓ Identification of the payer (payer).
- ✓ Identification of the beneficiary (debt collector).
- ✓ Amount of the transfer in numbers and letters.
- ✓ Currency in which the transfer is made.
- ✓ Identification of the foreign payer bank. Name and location of the bank where the beneficiary of the transfer has an account. Swift or bic code (international bank code). It is made up of 8 or 11 alphanumeric digits that contain the identification of the name and office of the bank and the country where it is located.
- ✓ Beneficiary's bank account number.

It must contain the identification numbers of the bank and branch where the money is destined. It should be borne in mind that the way banks and branches are coded in numbers is different in each country, and there is no single criterion. **Iban** (international account number). This is a European attempt to identify bank account numbers in

Europe in a similar way. The first two digits are those identifying the country (ES is Spain), the next two are control digits, and the rest is the complete account number that includes information on the name of the bank, the branch, and the individual account number.

- ✓ Statistical code or concept of the transfer, mandatory for payments over 12,500 euros. Required to justify the outflow of funds from the country to the Banco de España. This information is used to monitor the movement of money between residents and non-residents and the Ministry of Finance prepares the Balance of Payments and Receipts.
- ✓ Distribution of the bank charges for the transfer. For international payments, both the sending bank and the payer charge a fee for the transfer. There are three types of apportionment of bank charges between the payer and the payee:

> The vast majority of the world's banks work with the **swift** communication system **(Society of worldwide international financial Transactions)** and are assigned an identification code called a swift code.

- ✓ **SHA** (shared) charges. The originator pays the fees of his sending bank and the beneficiary pays the fees of his payer bank.
- ✓ **OUR** charges (on behalf of the payer). The payer pays his bank's charges and those of the foreign payer's bank. The beneficiary pays no charges.
- ✓ **BEN** charges (for the account of the beneficiary). The beneficiary pays his bank's charges and those of the bank issuing the transfer. The originator pays no charges.
- ✓ **Issuance of the transfer.** The issuing bank, if it considers the details of the payment order request to be sufficient, accepts the request and issues the transfer (payment order). It debits the payer's account for the amount in euro or in the currency equivalent, plus commissions where applicable. The payment information is sent to the foreign payment, and cleared via correspondent banks, or *target systems* (European central banks) or *eba,* depending on the case. The valuation of the transfer in euros is one day and in foreign currencies two days.
- ✓ **Receipt and crediting of funds.** The payer bank receives the funds from the transfer and credits them, net of fees where applicable, to the account of its customer who is the beneficiary of the transfer.

The following types of transfers can be encountered:

Transfers to the European Union. Law 9/1999 regulates payments within the European Union and in the currencies of its member countries. Its aim is to achieve an increase in the speed of payment and a reduction in banking costs, in order to bring them into line with national banking costs. To achieve this, it requires the use of all necessary bank details, including the Iban and the swift code, and penalises transfers with incomplete data.

Other transfers. These are transfers not regulated by Law 9/1999 on cross-border transfers in the European Union. The use of transfers in international trade operations involves a series of advantages and disadvantages.

☐ In terms of advantages we can cite:

➤ Easy to process. The payer only needs to provide the payee's full bank details, the amount and currency and the concept if it is a payment of more than 12,500 euros. Easy accessibility for both individuals and companies.
➤ Very secure means of payment. As it is made electronically, there is no risk of forgery or loss.
➤ A quick way of making a payment. There is no negotiation or collection management as with cheques, and there is a gain in agility over documentary means of payment.
➤ Low cost. Fees for transfers are small, similar to those for cheques, and cheaper than remittances or documentary credits.
➤ On the contrary, it has the following disadvantages:
➤ It does not cover the commercial risk of collection. In cases where the goods are delivered before payment is made, it depends on the seriousness of the importer to meet the payment deadline.

3.1.3. SIMPLE REMITTANCES

A *clean collection* is a means of payment whereby the exporter hands over a financial document to his bank for collection. The banks involved are responsible only for managing the collection on behalf of the exporter, within the framework of the rules established by the International Chamber of Commerce and good banking practices, without assuming any responsibility other than those of a technical nature.

This means of payment requires a certain amount of trust between buyer and seller, as the collection risk is not covered by the bank. It may happen that the exporter demands acceptance of the bill of exchange, but guaranteed by the importer's bank, making the simple remittance a bank guarantee through the financial bill of exchange. Here it is important that the foreign bank is internationally recognised to limit the banking risk.

We consider bills of exchange, promissory notes, cheques collected for collection, financial receipts and other similar documents as financial documents or bills of exchange. When the importer does not make payment on a consignment that he has previously accepted, the exporter can use this accepted financial document for claims before the competent court.

In Spain, bills of exchange such as bills of exchange, promissory notes issued without a "not to order" clause, and other documents that fulfil a draft function in international payments, must be stamped in order to comply with the law on property transfers and documented legal acts.

<u>The parties involved in a single consignment are:</u>

- ➢ Assignor. This is the exporter who delivers a financial document drawn in favour of the importer to his bank for collection. Unless otherwise instructed, the bank charges incurred in the remittance will be for his account.
- ➢ Exporter's bank (remitting bank). Bank that, according to the instructions received from its customer, forwards the financial document to the importer's bank in charge of collection.
- ➢ Importer's bank (presenting bank). Receives the remittance from the exporter's bank and presents it to the importer for collection.
- ➢ Drawee. This is the importer, who makes the payment according to his bank's instructions. Depending on the date of payment of the remittance, we distinguish between the following types of simple remittance:
- ➢ Payable on demand. The importer or drawee must pay the remittance when it is presented to him.
- ➢ Payable on time. Payment is made on a predetermined due date. Depending on the instructions of the exporter's bank, acceptance by the importer of the financial document may or may not be required.

The banking institutions involved shall be responsible solely for managing the collection on behalf of the exporter, within the framework of the rules laid down by the International Chamber of Commerce and good banking practice, without assuming any responsibility other than those of a technical nature.

This means of payment requires a certain amount of trust between buyer and seller, as the collection risk is not covered by the bank. It may happen that the exporter demands the acceptance of the bill of exchange, but guaranteed by the importer's bank, thus turning the simple remittance into a bank guarantee through the financial bill of exchange. Here it is important that the foreign bank is internationally recognised to limit the banking risk.

Financial documents or bills of exchange include bills of exchange, promissory notes, cheques in collection, financial receipts and other similar documents.

When the importer fails to make payment on a consignment he has previously accepted, the exporter can use that accepted financial document for claims before the competent court.

In Spain, bills of exchange such as bills of exchange, promissory notes issued without a "not to order" clause, and other documents that fulfil a draft function in international payments, must be stamped in order to comply with the law on property transfers and documented legal acts.

<u>The parties involved in a simple consignment are</u>:

- ➢ Assignor. This is the exporter who delivers a financial document drawn in favour of the importer to his bank for collection. Unless otherwise instructed, the bank charges incurred in the remittance will be for his account.
- ➢ Exporter's bank (remitting bank). Bank which, according to the instructions received from its customer, forwards the financial document to the bank.
- ➢ of the importer in charge of collection.
- ➢ Importer's bank (presenting bank). Receives the remittance from the exporter's bank and presents it to the importer for collection.
- ➢ Drawee. This is the importer, who makes the payment according to his bank's instructions.
- ➢ Depending on the date of payment of the remittance, we distinguish between the following types of simple remittances:
- ➢ Payable on demand. The importer or drawee must pay the remittance when it is presented to him.
- ➢ Payable on time. Payment is made on a predetermined due date. Depending on the instructions of the exporter's bank, acceptance by the importer of the financial document may or may not be required.

> Once the bill of exchange has been accepted, the document may remain with the beneficiary's bank or be returned to the exporter's bank and then presented again

> at the time of maturity for payment on demand. It is
> normally held by the importer's bank.

3.2. DOCUMENTARY MEANS OF PAYMENT

Documentary means of payment are the most secure, although they require the processing of commercial, transport or other documents between banks, and are more expensive. However, we can pass on the financial costs to our customers. Let us look at the main documentary means of payment:

3.2.1. DOCUMENTARY REMITTANCE

The documentary remittance or "***documentary collection***" is a means of payment made up of commercial documents and one or several financial documents, which an exporter delivers to its bank to manage its collection. Commercial documents are those that are not financial, the basis of Foreign Trade, the most commonly used commercial documents, invoice, transport document, insurance document, etc.) The parties involved in this means of payment are the same as in the simple remittance.

The documentary remittance is developed following the same procedure as for simple remittances, the only difference being that more types of documents appear in the documentary remittance:

- ➢ Delivery of documents from the exporter to his bank. When the exporter sends the goods to the importer, he goes to his bank with the commercial and financial documents that he has previously agreed with his foreign client, and gives instructions to his bank (remitting bank) on how to manage the collection, under what conditions and with which foreign bank. At the same time, he sends the goods in accordance with the terms and conditions of the sales contract.
- ➢ Sending the documentary remittance to the presenting bank. The exporter's bank or collecting bank, following its client's instructions, sends the documents to the presenting bank (importer's bank), attaching a cover letter indicating the characteristics of the consignment.
- ➢ Delivery of documents to the importer by his bank. The presenting bank makes the documents available to its client, the importer, who may collect them against payment or acceptance of the financial document. With the documents, the importer will proceed to collect the goods from customs when they arrive at their destination.

➢ Payment of the documentary remittance. Once the documents have been delivered to the importer, the presenting bank follows the instructions on the remittance and makes payment if the remittance is payable on demand or communicates acceptance of the bill of exchange if it is payable on time, making payment on maturity.

> If the importer does not accept the bill of exchange or does not withdraw the documents, his bank must inform the exporter's bank, which will inform its customer. If the documents are still not accepted, the collecting bank will request the return of the documents from the presenting bank.

<u>Documentary remittance has both advantages and disadvantages</u>:

✓ With regard to the advantages we find:
✓ This means of payment is cheaper than documentary credit.
✓ The exporter has the security of possession of the goods until such time as the importer makes payment or undertakes to do so by accepting the bill of exchange.
✓ The importer can obtain financing from the exporter if the shipment is deferred.
✓ On the other hand, it also has the following disadvantages:
✓ This payment system is not as secure as a documentary credit, where at least one bank guarantees the payment.
✓ The importer must take into consideration the possibility of falsification of documents.
✓ The importer cannot check the goods before accepting or making payment, so he has to rely on the documents.
✓ Where the importer does not agree to pay, the exporter would have to bear the costs of storage at the port or customs office of destination and the cost of transport in the case of return of the goods to the exporter's country.

The following legislation applies to documentary consignments:

Uniform Rules Relating to Collections, 1995 Revision, International Chamber of Commerce publication number 522. These are private rules issued by the International Chamber of Commerce. In order to apply these rules, it is necessary to put it in writing in the bank's covering letter with the characteristics of the remittance.

> A ruling by the International Chamber of Commerce on a dispute between the parties is not binding in the ordinary courts of a country, but can be used as a ruling by a panel of international trade experts.

3.2.2. DOCUMENTARY CREDITS

A documentary credit is the commitment that a financial institution acquires, at the request of its importer client and following its instructions, to guarantee the payment of goods to the exporter, against the delivery by the latter of certain required documents, which demonstrate that all the terms and conditions stipulated in this means of payment have been met.

The following spoke:

- **Originator.** This is the importing company that asks its bank to issue a documentary credit according to the instructions previously agreed with the exporter. It requests a foreign trade risk line from its bank in order to be able to issue the documentary credit or, if it has one, it checks that it has available risk.
- **Bank issuing the documentary credit.** Receives the credit application from its client, the originator, studies the risk and, if approved, proceeds to open the credit, informing the advising bank in the beneficiary's country via swift of the characteristics of the credit. Once the credit has been issued, the originator makes a firm commitment to make the payment under the agreed conditions.
- **Intermediary bank.** This is the bank to which the issuing bank turns when it issues the documentary credit. It receives the credit instructions and sends them either to the advising bank or directly to the beneficiary (if the intermediary bank coincides with the advising bank).
- **Advising bank.** Normally the bank where the exporter has an account. It receives the opening instructions from the intermediary bank and notifies the beneficiary of the opening. When the exporter delivers the documents, it checks them and sends them to the issuing bank. Depending on how the credit can be used, he can either initiate the collection of the credit or wait for the issuing bank to pay and then pay the beneficiary. Depending on whether it is payable at the cashier's office of the issuing bank or not.

- ➤ **Beneficiary.** This is the exporting company that receives the amount of the documentary credit in its favour. It will be responsible for obtaining the agreed documents and complying with the delivery conditions reflected in this means of payment.
- ➤ **Confirming bank.** In the event that the credit is confirmed, the confirming bank acquires the same obligations as the issuing bank.
- ➤ **Paying bank.** Depending on which bank initiates the payment (use of the credit) this paying bank function may be exercised by the following banks:
  - ✓ Issuing bank, if payable at its cashiers.
  - ✓ Advising bank, if payable at its cashiers.
  - ✓ Confirming bank, which adds its payment commitment, may be the advising bank.
  - ✓ Negotiating bank, where the credit is payable on a negotiable basis at a specific bank.
  - ✓ Any bank, where the credit is freely negotiable with any institution in a country.

<u>The documentary credit works as follows:</u>

- ✓ Application for the documentary credit. Once the importer has agreed with the exporter to pay for the goods by means of a documentary credit, the importer goes to his bank to request the issuance of the documentary credit. When issuing a documentary credit, the following aspects must be considered:
- ✓ Tolerance. In the amount, quantity, and unit price indicated, a difference of up to 5% more or less is allowed, and the percentage allowed must be specified. It ranges from 0 to 5 per cent.
- ✓ Place and deadline for submitting documents. Maximum date authorised for the required documents to arrive at the bank where they have to be checked and verified that the documents pre seated are as requested, and used (disposed of), i.e. once the documents have been checked, initiate payment or issue discrepancies (if the documents or delivery deadlines are not correct). The place of submission of documents refers to where the credit is to be used, i.e. where the paying bank is located.
- ✓ Places of origin and destination. Mention where the goods are leaving from and to which city they are destined for.
- ✓ Possibility of split shipments. If the exporter can make several shipments of the same order, all covered by a single documentary credit.
- ✓ Possibility of transhipment. This refers to whether the goods can change means of transport on the way to the destination or whether they must be on the same ship, lorry, wagon or aircraft at all times.
- ✓ Final date of shipment. Maximum date of departure of the goods from the point of origin.

<u>Methods of payment of documentary credits</u>:

- Payable on demand. Payment is made against presentation of documents to the importer, provided that all terms and conditions of the credit have been met.
- Deferred payment. Payment is made at a later date than the date of delivery of the documents. Normally the deadline is usually from the date of shipment of the goods (reflected in the transport document). It can also be from the date of issue of the invoice, date of delivery of the documents, or a date fixed in advance.
- Payment by acceptance. In this case there is a bill of exchange (bill of exchange) forming part of the documentary credit documents, and it will be necessary to accept it in order to make payment.
- Payment by negotiation. A financial bill of exchange is also used here, which can be discounted at a pre-designated negotiating bank, or in the case of a freely negotiable bill of exchange, any bank in the country where it is used can be a negotiating bank. This formula is rarely used in Europe, but is widely used in Eastern countries.
- ✓ Description of the goods. Indicate a brief description of the products and quantities purchased of the same, according to invoice or order.
- ✓ Documents required. Different commercial, transport, insurance and financial documents required from the exporter.
- ✓ Distribution of bank charges. Mention whether the bank charges both inside and outside Spain are for the account of the buyer or the seller. Most commonly, the bank charges in Spain are for the account of the Spanish company and the charges abroad are for the account of the foreign company.

Issuance of the documentary credit. Following the instructions indicated in the application for the documentary credit, the issuing bank notifies the intermediary bank, with which it has a relationship, of the issuance of the documentary credit. The intermediary bank, if different from the advising bank, communicates the issuing bank's issuance of the documentary credit to the advising bank.

> It is possible to modify the conditions for issuing the credit, always before the goods are dispatched. Each modification is requested by the issuing bank according to the instructions of the originator who has previously agreed with the beneficiary. Bank charges are incurred.

Notification of the opening of the credit to the exporter. The advising bank notifies the exporter of the opening of the documentary credit in his favour, its terms of delivery and the documents requested.

Dispatch of the goods and delivery of documents to the exporter's bank. Once the exporter has prepared the goods and the documents required in the documentary credit, the goods are dispatched to their destination and the documents are delivered to the advising bank, which will check them and send them to the bank paying the documentary credit.

Receipt of the documents by the paying bank and utilisation of the credit. This paying bank is responsible for checking whether the documents arrive before the deadline, whether they are the documents ordered, and whether the delivery conditions reflected in the documents are those agreed and reflected in the documentary credit. If everything is in order, he sends the documents to the originator, via the issuing bank (perhaps the same one, if the credit is payable at the cashier's office of the issuing bank) and follows the agreed payment instructions. When payment is made, the documentary credit is closed. If there are discrepancies with the documents presented or with the delivery terms or other conditions agreed in the credit, reservations are made, and the paying bank must communicate them to the issuing bank and the issuing bank to its customer, the payer, who will then decide whether or not to accept the credit despite the reservations. If the reservations are not accepted, the advising bank is informed so that the beneficiary is informed, the documents are returned and an attempt is made to correct the discrepancies (reservations) promptly. If not corrected, the documentary credit would not be paid.

> It should be mentioned that the issuing bank and the confirming bank, if any, is obliged to pay when the documents and conditions of the credit are respected, but they do not take into account the actual situation of the goods, in case it is different from the one reflected in the documents.

The following types of documentary credits can be found:

- **Irrevocable credits.** An irrevocable credit is one that cannot be cancelled or modified without the prior agreement of the parties involved. It represents an assurance given by the bank issuing the credit to the beneficiary that, if the beneficiary presents in due time documents according to the terms and conditions reflected in the credit, he will obtain the collection of the export at the agreed time. According to the UCP 600 rules, if there is no indication as to the revocability or irrevocability of the documentary credit, it is deemed to be irrevocable. Now in force UCP 600, July 2007.

- **Confirmed credits.** These are credits in which the issuing bank asks the advising or intermediary bank to add its confirmation, i.e. to make an irrevocable commitment to pay the documentary credit to the beneficiary. The requested bank may or may not accept the confirmation but is not obliged to do so. Therefore, in this type of credit there is a double guarantee of payment, one given by the issuing bank and the other by the confirming bank. Confirmed credits are used when there is a high-country risk.

- **Transferable credits.** The first beneficiary may require the bank authorised to pay, accept or negotiate to make the credit available, in whole or in part, to one or more second beneficiaries. The credit can only be transferable once, the second or second beneficiary(ies) cannot in turn designate third beneficiaries. The fact that the claim is transferable must be stated at the time the claim is issued. The conditions of the documentary credit are respected, the only things that can be modified are the amount, which can be reduced, and the period of validity, which can be shortened.

- **Stand-by credits.** A stand-by letter of credit is a guarantee from the issuing bank, which is honoured only when the importer does not make payment, i.e. does not pay directly by transfer, cheque or other means of payment. It is often used in some trade relations with the United States, as a guarantee of collection. They have their own ISP 98 regulation.

- **Back to back credits.** These credits are widely used by tradings and intermediaries, as they do not need to make two different credits in triangulated operations. With the export credit, they guarantee the import credit, as it will always be for a larger amount.

- **Revolving credits.** These are credits that offer financial availability and are automatically renewed. They can be cumulative or non-cumulative

- **Red" and "green" clause credits.** Allows the exporter to take advance payments before the goods are shipped. The importer finances him. The difference with the green clause is that it requires documentary justification for the advances.

- **Electronic credits and eUCPs.** Electronic documentary credits available since March 2002. They do not require a specific system such as EDI. The eUCP does not regulate the issuing and notification of a documentary credit. Allows submission in electronic format or mixed. In order for parties to submit to eUCP they must specify and indicate this via Swift by means of "EUCP" codes. This means of payment provides advantages to both the importer and the exporter, being the most accepted in situations of mutual ignorance, as it provides collection guarantees superior to those of any other form of payment.

The advantages are:
- ➢ Coverage of the commercial risk of collection. The exporter trusts in the solvency of the importer as there is a bank that is responsible for him and agrees to issue

him with a documentary credit. He knows that once the credit has been issued, he can manufacture the goods with the great certainty of being able to collect payment, provided that delivery is made according to the agreed conditions.

➤ Control of the conditions of delivery of the goods. When applying for credit, the importer informs about the time limit for the goods to leave the country, the places of origin and destination, how they are to be transported, and requests documents proving the correct disposition of the goods (transport, certificates of origin, insurance, list of contents, invoice). In addition, the importer has the guarantee that, if he pays, the bank will provide him with the documents that will allow him to clear the goods. The exporter is the owner of the goods until the importer accepts the agreed documents and collects the goods from customs with them.

➤ Possibility of improving payment conditions. The importer, by accepting payment by documentary credit, will be able to take advantage of this tool that ensures the exporter's collection to negotiate with him an improvement in the payment term, or a special discount.

➤ Possibility to request financing from the bank. The importer, when applying for the foreign trade line to open the credit, can use it to finance the payment of the credit.

> The importer must consider the delivery and document submission deadlines, the type of transport, the places of origin and destination of the goods, the documents to be requested, the distribution of bank charges, aspects that are not fully foreseen in transfers, cheques or remittances.

On the downside, we find:

➤ Complex processing. This is the most complete means of payment and with the greatest benefits for both the exporter and the importer of those we have seen, but it is also the most difficult to process, as it covers the conditions of delivery of the goods and those of payment. You must also apply for a foreign trade line from your bank if you do not have one. The exporter must obtain the requested documents within the agreed timeframe, and have the goods ready before the shipment deadline.

➤ High bank costs. As the payment is guaranteed at least by the bank issuing the credit, and the processing is more complex than other means of payment, the bank charges are also higher.

➤ Possibility of differences between the documents delivered and the goods received. As the documentary credit is a guarantee of payment by the issuing bank as long as certain conditions are met, the payment will be made if the documents are as requested, not if the goods are in order. Once the issuing bank delivers the documents to the orderer to collect the goods, it accepts the payment, guaranteed by the bank, and it may be that when checking the goods there are differences with the order, not reflected in the documents, which have to be solved between the buyer and the seller.

With regard to the legislation applicable to documentary credit, we find:

➢ Uniform Customs and Practice for Documentary Credits, of the International Chamber of Commerce, Publication 600, revision of 2007. Publication 600, revision 2007, July 1st marks the entry into force of the UCP 600. These are private rules issued by a private company, such as the International Chamber of Commerce, but generally accepted in all countries. They are not binding in the event of a legal dispute. These rules apply to all documentary credits as long as this is stated in the text of the credit.
➢ Honour or negotiate under UCP600.

Honour means:
✓ Pay on demand if the credit is available for payment on demand.
✓ Enter into a deferred payment commitment and pay at maturity if the credit is available for deferred payment.
✓ Accept a bill of exchange drawn by the beneficiary and pay at maturity if the credit is available for acceptance. A bill of exchange is only honoured if a promise to pay is given.
✓ What's new in the UCP 600:
✓ Payment and acceptance are grouped under a single category, which they call HONRA (Honour).
✓ It is understood that, in a credit available for deferred payment, the designated bank is required to promise payment.
✓ Negotiation is redefined and is no longer the only possible financing within the framework of credit.

4. INTERNATIONAL FUNDING

It is not very common for small and medium-sized companies to have experts in international finance, as their core business is to produce and sell value-added products and not to speculate with currencies. However, in this chapter, we will see a sea of possibilities in terms of financial products within the reach of many companies.

4.1. FACTORING

In recent years, the Spanish factoring market has seen a significant increase in its operations. From 2002 onwards, it began to exceed the 23% increase in activity. Approximately we are talking about 4.55% of GDP. When a company makes numerous sales on credit to its customers, it has to add the following vicissitudes to its productive activity:

- ✓ Manage and collect invoices issued.
- ✓ To cover the risk of possible insolvencies of its customers.
- ✓ To meet the liquidity or cash flow needs of the company, as payment deferrals tend to be lengthy.

Through this financing system, the company contracts a set of insolvency cover, management and financing services applicable to credit sales made to its customers, both in the domestic and international markets. These services are provided on the basis of the "*commercial assignment*" of invoices to a bank, the "factor".

- They make sales with deferred payment between 30 and 270 days. A clear example is the distribution of large chains, multinationals, public bodies, corporations, where payment terms are extended.
- They use transfer or cheque as a form of payment. We could also include those that use the promissory note or accepted draft, as the documents are sometimes late.
- They need insolvency cover for their sales, in addition to financing.
- They have a limited number of buyers, who represent a significant number of the turnover (80% and are 20% of the suppliers), which represents an excessive concentration of risks to be covered.
- Companies that are expanding and evolving, that need financing in order to grow.

> In the case of large companies, factoring allows them to improve their balance sheet structure by mobilising their trade receivables.

There are different types of factoring, depending on the services required by the company or the type of debtor that the company assigns to the bank.

According to the services offered to the client, we find the following:

Non-recourse factoring. The recipients are companies that sell to other companies and that, in addition to financing and the rest of the factoring services, want to ensure the collection of their credit sales and need to take out insolvency cover. The factor, on the other hand, performs the following services:

- ✓ Study and determine the maximum risk figure for each debtor (minimum sales per debtor are usually €100,000 and above).
- ✓ It monitors the portfolio.
- ✓ Manages collection.
- ✓ You can advance 80 to 95% of the amount of the invoices.
- ✓ Find out the causes of non-payment in the event of non-payment.
- ✓ It offers up to 100% insolvency risk coverage.

> In terms of **requirements,** the company must have repetitive and commercial term sales, with a maximum of 270 days. The assignment of all sales to the same debtor in favour of a single factoring entity (**globality of the assignment**).

Recourse factoring. Targets are small and medium-sized enterprises that need financing because they sell to large companies or multinationals that pay on a repo basis, or are excessively slow to have a negotiable document.

In terms of **services**, the factor usually performs:

- ✓ Classification of debtors according to credit limit granted
- ✓ Sales financing: advance payment of 80 to 95% of the invoice amount
- ✓ Control and accounting and statistical information on the assigned portfolio
- ✓ Collection management
- ✓ Management of unpaid debts
- ✓ Depending on the debtor:

Domestic private sector factoring. In terms of its characteristics, the debtor is located in the national territory. The globality of the assignment is required and it **can be with or without recourse**.

Factoring private sector export. The debtor is outside the national territory. The intervention of a second factor, located in the country of importation, is normally necessary. **The operations are always without recourse.**

In terms of **advantages for the exporter**, we can cite the following:

✓ It removes uncertainties when considering international expansion.
✓ It has immediate financing for all its sales to importers (previously classified and approved) pending collection and previously assigned to the bank.
✓ It is fully protected against the risk of insolvency of those buyers previously classified.
✓ It eliminates long payment periods, bureaucratic and legislative obstacles in different countries.
✓ It benefits from specialised foreign collection management, as it is carried out by an entity in the importing country itself. The **advantages for the importer are as follows:**
✓ No need to provide guarantees
✓ You do not need documentary credits to make payments; it is sufficient to receive the goods in the condition and according to the documentation presented.

Public sector factoring. In terms of characteristics, the debtor is a central, regional or local administration, university, public or mixed capital companies (TVE, RENFE, hospitals, Social Security, etc.). The assignment to the factor and its corresponding approval is usually done **invoice by invoice** or certification by certification. It can be with or without recourse. In general, it allows companies, regardless of their financial structure, to develop and grow with security, insofar as their customers are worthy of the risks arising from the sale of invoices on credit.

Another advantage would be the decongestion of the administration of the companies because they do not have to:

➢ Conduct credit rating of buyers.
➢ Assume the risk of insolvency.
➢ Find ways to finance sales on credit.
➢ Managing collections.
➢ To carry out the accounting control of the invoice portfolio.

It is a method of automatically financing your sales in line with the company's growth or internationalisation. By factoring "without recourse", the company reduces its trade receivables, which allows it to improve its solvency and its return on assets ratio (ROA). Moreover, it assumes no risk of being listed in the CIRBE (Central Risk Register of the Bank of Spain). In times of crisis and lack of liquidity in companies, it should be a means of financing that should be seriously considered. Below is an example of the rates for factoring operations:

✓ Administration and formalisation costs.
✓ Opening .... 1502,53 €
✓ Study .... 60,10€
✓ Litigation proceedings. 30,05€
✓ Subscription notes ...... 30,05€

> ✓ Factoring fees.
> ✓ Factoring without recourse (2%) with a minimum of €12.02.
> ✓ Factoring with recourse (1.7%) minimum of €10.02.

4.2. FORFAITING

Forfaiting or **non-recourse discounting consists of** the sale of financial documents, with medium-term maturities, corresponding to the payment of exported goods and services, without recourse against the exporter.

The transaction is carried out at a price that represents the present value of future maturities, discounted. This technique, which is very quick to execute, is characterised by being:

Abstractable: whatever documentation is used, it must allow separation between the rights acquired with the purchase of the instrument and the commercial transaction that gave rise to its issuance. This means that neither the debtor nor the guarantor bank can use defaults, commercial disputes or other incidents as an excuse to refuse payment of the debt.

Negotiable: The claims which are the subject of a transaction must be freely transferable.

Commercial: In a forfaiting transaction the credit arises because of a contract for the sale of goods and therefore qualifies as a commercial credit.

Without recourse: Once the transaction has been completed, the seller can completely disengage himself from the events affecting the assigned claim, while the buyer has no possibility of returning the claim to the seller in the event of non-payment by the debtor, except in the case of fraud. In the case of a definitive sale, the payment instruments used must necessarily involve an unconditional and irrevocable promise to pay. The most frequently used are: **promissory notes, bills of exchange and letters of credit with deferred payment**, preferably with acceptance. However, documents such as commercial invoices, claims under a supply contract, etc. may also be discounted without recourse, provided that they offer sufficient certainty of the right to demand payment of the obligation at maturity. The vast majority of transactions discounted on the forfaiting market involve some form of bank guarantee. On the one hand, this reduces the credit risk and speeds up the forfaiter's analysis process. On the other hand, it increases the liquidity of the asset on the secondary market. However, a growing number of companies, large corporations, well known in the international markets, are nowadays widely accepted names that do not need any additional collateral, although it always depends on the economic situation we are living in. In the current situation, guarantees are multiplying. For a guarantee to be suitable for forfaiting, it must be: **unconditional, irrevocable and transferable**.

> Both promissory notes and bills of exchange are transferred by endorsement, which in its simplest form consists of the signature of the beneficiary of the instrument on the back of the instrument. **Endorsement** without recourse conveys the right to receive payment of the bill, but not the right of recourse to the seller in the event of non-payment.

It is important that the wording of the document leaves no doubt as to the validity of the obligation and that the guarantee is legally enforceable. The most commonly used form of security in the forfaiting market is the **surety**.

The elements that normally make up the cost of a forfaiting operation are:

☐ <u>Discount Fee</u>: quoted as a margin above the LIBOR rate which depends on its duration: 6 months, 18 months, etc.

☐ <u>Days of Grace: or the </u>number of days that forfaiters add to each maturity in the maturity calculation.

☐ <u>Commitment fee: this is </u>the fee charged by the forfaiter for reserving sufficient credit lines and country risk to be able to carry out a given transaction under certain conditions. Although there are no precise rules, the commitment fee is usually around 50% of the margin.

From the point of view of an exporting company, forfaiting achieves several objectives:

✓ Liquidity.
✓ Reduction of credit, exchange rate and interest rate risks.
✓ Maintenance of credit lines with banks.
✓ Improvement of accounting ratios.
✓ Savings in paperwork and time.
✓ Interest and commissions are a deductible expense for corporate and personal income tax purposes.

It is important that these characteristics are taken into account when comparing the cost of forfaiting with other financing alternatives. In particular, it is not unusual for companies, especially small and medium-sized ones, to find forfaiting expensive because they compare it with the discounting of bills with recourse offered by their usual bank or savings bank. For certain transactions, the use of forfaiting as a financing alternative is not a viable way forward.

> An alternative to a guarantee is a **bank guarantee**, which is permitted in a separate document from the promissory note or bill of exchange. Each bank usually has its own format, and the text can range from a few lines to several pages where various legal aspects are considered in detail.

Also, in the case of operations that lend themselves to being supported by the ECESB, forfaiting is not usually a suitable alternative unless:

- ✓ The contract needs to be signed urgently.
- ✓ The importer does not want to get involved in the operational and administrative complexity of an officially supported operation.
- ✓ The contract is already in the execution phase.

However, there are many situations in which it would be appropriate to consult this market to verify the availability of credit and its cost. For exports of machinery or other capital goods, which provide for medium-term payment, where credit can be evidenced by promissory notes or other transferable instruments, it is always worth asking for a quotation. The earlier the price is requested, the easier it will be to include the cost of the discount in the value of the commercial contract.

Similarly, for a company with limited access to the banking market, forfaiting can be attractive in terms of both availability and cost. Forfaiting allows some flexibility in determining when to access the market. An exporter can decide to keep the credit on its books for a certain period of time or to sell only part of the credit. The forfaiting market lends itself to creating tailor-made products. So do not be afraid to propose different operations to the market. The local bank used by the exporter often plays an important role in suggesting or discarding the use of the product. An institution that knows the market well can advise on how best to structure the transaction and how to find the best price.

> Transactions below €500,000 are not very attractive for many forfaiters, especially when the number of maturities is high. This is not only because of the limited profit potential, but also because of the difficulty of hedging the interest risk and the high administrative cost. Even if a bid is successful, the price may be very high. In the following, we will look at an example of forfaiting finance system fees. In discounting with recourse or forfaiting, fees are usually charged:
>
> ☐ Management fee .... 2%.
>
> ☐ Annual commitment fee .... 1%.

4.3. PROJECT FINANCE

Project finance is an innovative financing mechanism that allows the promoter of a public or private project to carry it out by obtaining the necessary investment financing without having to resort to own or external resources. Unlike the credit mechanisms normally used, *project finance* is based fundamentally on the project's capacity to generate resources, which must be sufficient to pay the returns on capital, the exporter's profit, as well as to repay the capital invested. The novelty is that the financial system replaces the traditional real guarantees with a multitude of reports and feasibility studies (technical, economic, legal, etc.), in addition to the contractual involvement of those involved in the development and management of the project. The guarantees end up being of the same importance and rank, but provided jointly and severally by a group of agents.

The viability of the project and its very low risk will be mandatory conditions for using this system. One of the main advantages of this type of financing is that it is done "off-balance sheet", without increasing the corporate and financial risks of the promoter companies, since the financial resources are lent against the project itself and are recovered through the cash generated by the project.

The scope of application is quite broad, as it can be used for purely private projects, as well as projects that are private through an administrative licence, a public concession, or fully public projects. The most suitable projects for this financing system are those which, due to their characteristics, require high initial investments and subsequently generate a secure and regular income. An example would be transport, renewable energies and energy use (waste treatment, recycling, biomass, wind and solar energy, etc.), water treatment, telecommunications, industrial and environmental projects, mining. As we can see, most current R&D&I projects can be eligible for this type of funding. In order for this financing to be offered "off-balance sheet", it is necessary to set up a structure independent of the promoter and with its own legal personality. This structure is known as a "Project Company" (PE), which will be the owner of the project assets and will bear the main risk of the operation.

This company must comply with the commercial and labour laws of the Spanish State and the European Union. It must also be flexible in terms of accepting new partners, accessing bank loans, limiting the liability of its partners to assets only. It must be privately and publicly controlled. All the entities that collaborate in the project, industrial partners that provide experience in the sector and financial partners that lend capital in the expectation of a return can participate in its constitution.

> The sources of funding for this model are varied: from long-term bank loans, to bonds and debenture issues, to grants from national or international agencies.

There is no general structure for such funding, as it depends on the type of project conditions. However, it is possible to speak of some standard structures:

- ➢ EP formed by private promoters who implement a project, operate it for a certain period of time and finally return it to the public sector. These are generally projects based on an _administrative concession_.
- ➢ Establishment of a PE made up of private and public promoters, where they jointly and severally assume the risks. Normally, once it is operational, the public sector no longer assumes the risks.
- ➢ Incorporation of a SOE with fully public capital, carrying out projects that generate constant revenue streams, e.g. tolls. In these cases, the construction and operation of the project can be carried out by either a public or a private entity through an administrative concession. Due to its complexity, it is necessary to have qualified external advisors, perfectly measuring the risks, so that investors and financial institutions have confidence in the project:

- ➢ _Engineering consultant_: they carry out the technical study.
- ➢ _Environmental impact assessor_: analyses the social and environmental impact of the project.
- ➢ _Financial advisor_: carries out a study of the profitability of the project, assessing the financial and economic risks, advising on the raising of resources to negotiate with financial institutions.

- ➢ <u>Legal advisor</u>: advises on all legal and fiscal aspects affecting the project.
- ➢ All revenue streams and project costs must be secured through a series of contracts:

Technical contracts:

- • <u>Construction phase</u>: turnkey installation contract, if this modality is chosen, supply of machinery, technical advice, etc.
- • <u>Operating phase</u>: contracts for the supply of raw materials, maintenance, etc.

Financial contracts:

- ✓ Financing during construction.
- ✓ Financing of the operating period.
- ✓ Insurance.

The construction phase involves the procurement of a large amount of capital equipment, civil works and various individual contracts. If it is ***turnkey***, the builder is responsible for the entire phase. It is the most widely accepted because financial institutions do not want to take risks. If the completion deadline is breached, there is a penalty.

If the "cost ***plus profit***" construction contract is chosen, it will be the EP that will be responsible for and bear the construction risks. The cost will be lower and only the design and construction of the project is paid for, with no additional costs. In these cases, financial institutions usually ask for more guarantees.

Normally, the bank that handles the administrative and management relations with the rest of the pool and the company executing the project is the one that assumes the greatest risk in the operation (as is the case in syndicated loans). In this case, it would be the TRM Bank, which provides 35% of the financing. In the jargon of Project Finance, the company executing the project is called SPV (Special Purpose Vehicle), which normally forms part of the project, although it does not necessarily have to exist for its development. The motorway construction project is structured in different phases, to each of which an amount of investment is assigned. In each phase, each financial institution in the pool is responsible for contributing the percentage described above, and would therefore also assume the proportion of that risk.

In addition, this type of project has an increasingly important social function, as the state is turning the construction of certain infrastructures over to private companies, which in practice becomes a way of allowing private capital to enter into large state investment projects.

Investment projects make a very valuable contribution to the financial economy, as many of the projects currently being carried out would not come to fruition if there were no entities willing to cooperate with each other in order to share risks. Not only because of the large amount of financing required, but also because of the diversification of risks in a large financial operation.

4.4. FAD CREDITS

The ADF was the first Spanish development aid instrument created in 1976. A credit can be considered an ADF if it meets the criteria set by consensus in the OECD, the "*Helsinki package*", credit lines on behalf of IMF members.

The FAD finances the amount of Spanish capital goods and services exported to developing countries, including freight and transport insurance contracted from a Spanish company and the export credit insurance premium (CESCE). It also finances the amount of foreign goods and services incorporated into the project. This item may not exceed 15% of the total of exported goods and services, both Spanish and foreign. It is usually complemented by a commercial credit, which is usually supported by the CESCE. The risk of covering the interest is covered by the ICO (Official Credit Institute), through the system of the Reciprocal Interest Adjustment Contract (CARI). Through the CARI, private financial institutions are encouraged to grant long-term export credits (from 2 years) at fixed interest rates. These minimum rates, known as Consensus or CIRR rates, are regulated by the OECD.

The CARI application is submitted to the ICO by the credit institution that will finance the export operation. In principle, all applications require authorisation by the Directorate General for Trade and Investment of the Ministry of Economy. If the operation complies with the general rules of the CARI, it is considered to be authorised on a generic basis and the ICO, on behalf of the Directorate General, issues an offer of terms and conditions directly to the lending institution. It is valid for a maximum period of 6 months. The FAD credit agreement between Spain and the recipient country may incorporate repayment rules in the form of compulsory purchase of Spanish goods and services. The DAC (Development Assistance Committee) then classifies it as tied aid.

As for the conditions of the process, the official request must be made by the authorities of a developing country. Spanish companies can submit their enquiries to the Directorate General for Trade and Investment of the Ministry of Economy.

The approval of each FAD financing is made by the Government, by agreement of the Council of Ministers, at the proposal of an inter-ministerial Commission created for this purpose (CIFAD). The ICO, as the State's financial agent, negotiates, signs and administers the FAD financing agreements.

Disbursement is made in accordance with the milestones established in the contract. Thus, the company is paid directly by the ICO as it provides documentary evidence of compliance with the contract, subject to acceptance by the beneficiary country. Compliance with the ICO is verified by a financial institution, known as the paying bank, previously selected by the beneficiary and approved by the ICO.

Since its inception, more than 85 countries have received ADF projects. The total amount of aid is almost €8 billion, with China, Morocco and Mexico being the main recipients, followed by Argentina, Algeria and Indonesia.

4.5. FINANCIAL INSTRUMENTS FOR IMPORTS AND EXPORTS

Both the exporter and the importer may finance their operations:

> **In your national currency**: In the case of a Spanish company in Euros.
> **In a different currency**: In the currency agreed in the sale and purchase, other than the national currency.
> **In a third currency**: trying to find a reduced interest rate.

> *If the exchange rate of the currency varies*, when you have to cancel the financing, it may have become more expensive (the exchange rate variation has been detrimental to you) or cheaper (the variation has been to your advantage).

Export financing: the exporter will seek to repay the financing requested with the funds received from the importer.

Import financing: the importer will try to repay with the proceeds from the sale of the imported goods. If he sells it on the domestic market (€), so financing in another currency will carry an exchange rate risk.

When the company is exposed to exchange rate risk, it can:

- **Assume**: if the expected evolution of the exchange rate will be in your favour, making your financing cheaper, but you run the risk of the opposite happening.
- **Eliminate it**: you would have to contract some financial hedging instrument (forwards, options, swaps, etc.). The most appropriate thing to do is to eliminate it.

4.5.1. EXPORT FINANCING

When we carry out an export activity, the terms are not usually in cash. Therefore, in order to achieve liquidity, companies finance themselves. The following scenarios are encountered:

The currency of payment and financing is the Euro. In this case there is no exchange rate risk. *"A company is going to be paid in 90 days. The amount of its sale is €6,000 and while it is financed with a credit of €6,000. At maturity, it will use the €6,000 collected to pay off the loan, without being affected in the slightest by the rate movement".*

The currency of collection is the Dollar and the currency of financing is the Euro. In this case there is RISK. *"The company is going to collect for the sale of 6,000 US$ and while it is financed with a credit of 4,878 €, with an exchange rate of 1.23$ = 1 €. The maturity date arrives after 90 days and the exchange rate is 1.25$ = 1 €, therefore, it will be able to exchange them for 4,800 €, it will have to return the credit and pay 78 € more. If the new rate were $1.19, he would receive €5,042, so he would earn €164.*

When the currency of collection and financing is the dollar: NO RISK. *"If the company is going to collect $5,000 in 90 days and in the meantime requests financing of $5,000, at maturity it will use this amount without being affected by possible movements in the exchange rate".*

4.5.2. FINANCING IMPORTS

To avoid decapitalisation, companies finance their purchases in order not to lose liquidity and to take advantage of discount opportunities. When the purchase is made in foreign currency, there is an exchange rate risk. These are the different situations that can arise:

- If you finance in the same currency in which the sale is made: there is NO EXCHANGE RISK. You will always get more on the sale than the amount financed.
- If it is financed in a currency other than that in which its sales are made: YES there is exchange RATE RISK.

4.5.3. FINANCIAL INSTRUMENTS FOR FOREIGN EXCHANGE RISK

Exchange rate risk can be accepted or eliminated: if accepted it can affect positively or negatively.

The most commonly used financial instruments are:

Forwards. The forward contract allows the exporter / importer to **hedge the exchange rate risk**: It is the purchase / sale of a currency at a fixed term and at a fixed exchange rate. The purchase/sale of the currency will take place when the agreed term arrives (e.g. 180 days) but the exchange rate agreed at the time of the forward contract will then be applied.

If the €/$ exchange rate changes during this period, they will not be affected, as they have already agreed with their financial institution on a certain exchange rate.

The **forward exchange rate** is a **different** exchange rate from the spot exchange **rate** we are all familiar with. The **forward exchange rate** is formed from the spot exchange rate and taking into account the interest rates of the two currencies being exchanged and the term of the transaction.

Figure 1. Forward exchange formula

$$\textbf{Forward exchange rate} = \text{Spot exchange rate} * \frac{1 + [\text{interest rate } € * (\text{no. days} / 365)}{1 + [\text{interest rate } \$ * (\text{no. days} / 365)}$$

The forward exchange rate is quoted on the markets, so that, in addition to the current exchange rate, forward exchange rates for different maturities (90, 180, 365 days, etc.) can be obtained by consulting a business newspaper.

Contracting a forwards:

- ➢ The exporter can close today the sale of the Euros it will receive in the future.
- ➢ The importer can close the purchase of the dollars he will need in the future.
- ➢ In this way, the exporter will know today how many Euros he will receive when he exchanges the dollars he has to be paid, for example in 90 days' time, for a sale made, and the importer will know how many Euros he will need to buy in the future the dollars with which to pay for the import he has made.

Another financial instrument that allows the exporter and importer to eliminate exchange rate risk. It gives the acquirer the right to buy/sell a currency at a future point in time at a given price.

> The option can be exercised or not, depending on whether or not it suits the holder. This is the first difference with forwards, in which **the holder is obliged to buy/sell the currency at the agreed exchange rate, once the maturity date has arrived, regardless of whether the exchange rate is favourable or not at that time.**

The following options are available:

<u>Call option:</u> gives the right to buy a currency at a future date at a fixed price. "*Option to buy US\$ 10,000 within 90 days at €0.80/US\$. At maturity, if the €/US\$ exchange rate stands at €0.81, the purchaser of the option will exercise it and buy the \$ at €0.80/US\$*". "*If, on the other hand, the exchange rate is €0.79, then he will not exercise his option, as it will be cheaper to buy the \$ at €0.79*".

<u>Put option:</u> Gives the right to sell a currency at a future date at a fixed price. "*Option to sell US\$ 10,000 within 90 days at €0.80. At maturity, if the exchange rate is €0.81, the purchaser of the option will not exercise it, as he can sell his \$ at €0.81*". "*If the exchange rate is €0.79, then he will exercise his option and sell at €0.80*". The exporter is going to receive foreign currency in the future, so he can buy a put option that allows him to sell that currency.

CONCLUSIONS

Before making an investment abroad, a company should consider whether there are tax incentives to do so, because, if there are, the return will be higher than expected. Take into account taxation, profit repatriation, etc. Taxes are recorded differently, especially VAT, whether we are talking about third countries, i.e. export and import, or intra-Community market, deliveries or acquisitions.

In the international environment, it is logical that in the first negotiations there is a risk of uncertainty in collection. Simple means of payment should therefore be used with companies that already have a long trading history. For the first steps, it is recommended to use documentary means of payment, especially documentary credit.

Factoring and forfaiting provide a system of international financing that is also a guarantee of collection. Financial instruments such as forwards and options help the company to reduce the risks of currency fluctuations. The company nowadays must provide itself with information regarding the strategies it is going to adopt with respect to the taxation of the destination countries. Especially if you are thinking of setting up a commercial or production branch or subsidiary.

As far as the European Union market is concerned, since the establishment of the Common Market, fiscally speaking, there have been changes in the fiscal treatment of taxes, especially VAT. We have abandoned customs documents for fiscal and control documents such as Intrastat, changes that have been generated as a result of an intra-Community market and third countries. Due to the insecurity generated by a different culture, different ways of understanding the business world, banks, in their eagerness to standardise their products, offer a series of payment and financial methods with a high level of collection security and guarantees.

ABOUT THE AUTHOR

José-Nicanor Pinilla Barcelona comes from a village in Zaragoza, Spain, Brea de Aragón, where shoes have been manufactured for generations. This has influenced his business outlook and entrepreneurial spirit. He has a business career of more than 30 years, and as a teacher and consultant in international trade, since learning by teaching is his main vocation. For more information visit LinkedIN profile: https://www.linkedin.com/in/escueladelemprendedor/